The Spice of

Spice Up Your Life With Thai Curry Pastes, Marinades, Rubs, Sauces, and Other Concoctions

Urassaya Manaying

TABLE OF CONTENTS

INTRODUCTION

If you've ever been to an authentic Thai restaurant, you already know that Thai food is all about a delicious balance between the five flavors- sweet, sour, salty, spicy, and bitter. Most recipes contain at least one ingredient for each of these flavors. Once you get used to Thai cooking, you will get a hang of Thai ingredients. You will get a sense of what ingredient does what, and how much of it you like in a particular recipe. You will then see the recipes in this book as a blank canvas, and tweak them to your, or your family's preferences. Let your instincts guide you, once you get a hang of things.

Each dish has a balance of ingredients, but a Thai meal too needs to be balanced as a whole, with a good variety of dishes that complement each other. For instance, if you're cooking a spicy curry, you will do well to serve a plain vegetable stir-fry on the side. It is also common for the Thai dinner table to have a few common taste making condiments so the individuals having the dinner can tweak the flavor of any dish to their liking. For example, vinegar, tamarind water and lime juice are common sour ingredients on the Thai dinner table.

Thai people enjoy food with a wide spectrum of ingredients, including seafood, meat, fruit, and vegetables. Here in Thailand, we like to enjoy what is in season, and what is available at hand in the kitchen. If we're short on an ingredient, we usually improvise.

You might find a few ingredients in this book that are hard to find. When in doubt, google the ingredient, and find a substitution. Some of the greatest recipes in the world are known to us today because someone, somewhere, improvised! So, feel free to improvise yourself. I know you'll need to.

Also, the amount of ingredients used are to my personal taste. Feel free to tweak any taste making ingredient to your own personal taste if you find the flavor too strong or too bland. It is always a good idea to start with less, as more spice can be added later, but it is impossible to remove it once it is in. You'll know the quantities you need to throw in for best results, after you've cooked a recipe once or twice.

Each recipe has "Yield" mentioned at the end. These are approximate, and since we Thai people like to enjoy multiple dishes in one meal, one serving of one dish might not be enough to satiate your hunger. Most recipes in this book are meant to be accompanied by rice.

The most important thing is to enjoy the process of Thai cooking. Follow your instincts, and let your creativity run wild!

WEATHER

Thailand enjoys a monsoon climate. The peninsula has two seasons: wet from November-July, and dry from August-October.

The mainland has three seasons: wet from May-November, dry and cool from November-February, and dry and hot from March-April. If you're from a cold country, however, you might say that the weather here is hot and humid all year round.

AGRICULTURE

Thailand's fertile delta region is complemented by its hot and humid climate, yielding perfect agricultural conditions. Some archeologists even believe that central Thailand was the site of the first true agriculture on the planet and that rice has been cultivated there since between 4000 and 3500 B. C. Agricultural products make up 66 percent of the country's exports, and produces more than a third of the world's rice. Other prominent products are coconut, tapioca, rubber, sugar, pineapple, jute, soybeans, and palm oil. Two-thirds of the Thai labor force is engaged in agriculture.

FOOD CULTURE

As we talked before, Thai food is all about balancing sweet, salty, sour, bitter, and hot flavors. Not only the dishes, but the whole meal needs to be balanced with a delicious combinations of all these flavors. A few of the most popular taste makers and flavoring agents in Thai cooking are: coconut, lime, chili, garlic, ginger, cilantro, and dried fish (to make fish sauce). These ingredients are the foundation of Thai flavors.

As with food of any other region, Thai food has a few foreign influences. Chilies were introduced to Asia by the Portuguese in the 16th century, and this hot ingredient became a favorite of the Thai people, and a staple in the Thai kitchen. Hence, the Portuguese have had a huge influence on Thai cuisine. China and their stir-frying cooking techniques too have had a great influence on Thai cuisine. Indian curries and Indonesian spices are quite popular here too.

Thailand enjoys a huge coastline, making seafood a staple. Freshwater fish are super popular here too. Fish sauce is an indispensable part of Thai cuisine, and is used as a sauce, condiment, salt substitute, general taste maker, and flavoring agent. Dried fish are a popular snack in the country.

The country has a tropical climate, which leads to a limitless supply of delicious and exotic fruits and vegetables that are used in pretty much every kind of dish, and sometimes eaten by themselves too. The most important agricultural produce of Thailand is rice. Rice is also the most important and most common ingredient in Thai cuisine. In Thailand, the white and fragrant rice varieties are considered the best. Jasmine rice is a long-grained rice that is one of the favorite varieties here.

Most of the people in Thailand are Theravada Buddhists, and for them killing of animals is forbidden, but eating them is allowed. Regardless, meat is not a very common ingredient in the Thai

isine, and is considered by most a special and rare treat. The
eat that is served is often shredded.

Thailand, all courses are usually served at once, so that the
ok can enjoy the meal with his/her guests. Condiments such as
ied chilies, chili paste, chopped peanuts, soy sauce, fish sauce,
c. are present on the table so the diners can tweak the flavor of
dish if they wish to.

aded with fish, vegetables, fruits, and rice, and low in meats
d dairy, Thai cuisine is one of the healthiest in the world. Thai
od is rich in carotinoids, flavonoids, and antioxidative vitamins,
known to have anti-cancer properties. It is no surprise that the
ai have the lowest rates of digestive tract cancer in the world.

HAI COOKING BASICS

fore we dive into the recipes, let us take a look at a few
idelines that might make your cooking experience a little
tter. These are quite basic, and if you've had some experience
following cookbooks in the past, you can skip them.

1. Read the recipe completely at least once before you start.
2. Make sure you have all the ingredients and tools needed
   for the recipe ready before you begin.
3. Fresh seasonal ingredients are always best.

4. Do all the cutting, chopping, and weighing the ingredients before you begin cooking.
5. Homemade ingredients are almost always better than store bought ones.
6. When measuring dry ingredients, level them off using the straight edge of a knife.
7. Use standard measuring spoons, cups, etc.
8. Rinse all vegetables and fruits meticulously and pat or spi dry.
9. Take meat out of the fridge approximately 15 minutes before cooking it, letting it come to room temperature. It will cook faster and more uniformly.
10. Use freshly ground pepper, if possible. Pepper starts to lo its flavor and pungency the moment it is ground.

BASIC COOKING METHODS

Here we will discuss a few of the most common cooking method used in Thai cooking. Thai cooking is usually quite simple, and th methods used here are not much different from those used in th rest of the world.

STIR-FRYING AND SAUTÉING

These are identical cooking techniques that involve cooking in a open pan over high temperatures and with a negligible amount cooking oil. Sautéing is usually done in either a slope-sided gourmet pan (or frying pan) or a straight-sided sauté pan. Stir-frying done in a wok.

These techniques are great for browning all kinds of meats.

Cooking fats must be relatively tasteless and have a high point. My favorites are canola oil and peanut oil. The oil must but not be smoking before you start to cook. To check, you can drizzle drop or two of water into the pan: It should spatter. Please be cautious as spatters can burn! Shaking the pan for sautéing or swiftly tossing ingredients in stir-frying prevents the food from adhering while it sears.

GRILLING AND BROILING

Grilling and broiling are cooking techniques in which food is cooked by exposing it to direct (often intense) heat over hot coals or some other heat source. This method is usually fast; the direct heat chars surface of the food, imparting delicious flavor to it. The fuel used in a grill impart a nuance of flavor. Adding aromatic wood chips such as or applewood or certain herbs such as lemongrass or fennel will impart additional flavor tones. (This cannot be done when using a broiler.)

The grill can be old fationed, using some type of charcoal, or an electric one. The best grills will allow for fairly controllable heat. To ready your grill for cooking, heat it until hot and then use a long-handled brush to scrape away any residue. Immediately before placing food on the grill, rub a wad of paper towels dipped in oil onto the grate. This will greatly reduce sticking.

Pretty much everything edible can be grilled: soft cuts of meat, poultry, game birds, seafood, fish, or vegetables. The food will grill more uniformly if you let it come to room temperature immediately before cooking. Seasoning, especially with salt, must be done just before you cook, as salt tends to draw out moisture, rendering your final product less juicy. Furthermore, foods that are naturally low in fat must be brushed with oil or butter coated with a sauce to keep them from drying out. Marinades are way to put in additional flavor to grilled foods.

To test when your grilled meat is done, it is best to use an instant thermometer. If you don't like this method, you can insert the point of a knife to visually see if your food is done. Always bear in mind that your food carries on cooking even after you take it off the grill. Furthermore, meats will reabsorb some of their juices after they are done cooking. Make sure you let your meats rest for 5-10 minutes before you serve.

COOKING IN WATER

Simmering and poaching are both techniques that involve cooking food in liquid. With both techniques, the cooking liquid is first brought a boil and then the heat is decreased in order to reduce bubbling. Poaching should have a little less bubbling ction than simmering, but it's hard to tell when something is simmering versus poaching. Some recipes require a covered cooking vessel, others open ones. As something is simmering or poaching, it is vital to skim surface regularly to remove the residue that accumulates. Fish, rice, and poultry all do great with poaching and simmering.

Only a few foods need to be boiled — noodles and potatoes being two of the most common ones. Boiling water is also used to blanch or parboil fruits vegetables before they are moved to another cooking method. Blanching involves placing the ingredients in boiling water for a short period of time and then immersing them into cold water to retain color and flavor or to make it easier to take their skins off. Ingredients that parboiled actually stay in the boiling water a small amount longer, in order to slightly tenderize them.

Another popular cooking technique involving water is steaming. With this method, the ingredients are not immersed in the water, but instead above it on a rack. The pot is covered at all times. Steaming is a very gentle cooking method and it is usually the most healthy. Steamed ingredients do not lose much of their nutrients, texture, or individual flavor. Vegetables and sticky rice do great with steaming.

ROASTING

Roasting is another fundamental cooking method used around the world. A very simple technique that requires an oven, usually with high heat. This technique can also use indirect heat from a grill to obtain similar results. Pretty much everything can be roasted: meats, fishes, vegetables, or fruits.

Roasting meat requires you to season it in some way, sometimes searing it before you place it in your oven and sometimes coating it it cooks — depending on the recipe — and always letting it rest Resting allows the meat to reabsorb some of its juices, making your roast juicy and easier to carve. To rest your roast, you simply remove it the oven, cover it using foil, and allow it to sit.

A useful gadget to have when roasting is an ovenproof meat thermometer. This will allow you to know when your roast is done to your preference, without cutting into it. For an accurate reading, you must insert tip of the thermometer into the deepest part of the meat without touching bone, fat, or the bottom of the pan. Roasting charts commonly come with the thermometers.

HANDY TOOLS FOR THAI COOKING

KNIFE TYPES AND THEIR USES

- **CHEF'S KNIFE** — a medium-bladed knife used for chopping cutting, mincing

- **PARING KNIFE** — a short-bladed knife (usually 2 to 4 inches) used trim fruits and vegetables
- **SLICING KNIFE** — a long-bladed knife, either smooth-edged or serrated used for cutting meats or breads

her useful knives include: boning, utility, cleaver, and fillet.

PECIALTY UTENSILS

you're getting started with Thai cooking and don't wish to
vest any more cash on fancy tools for the job, you will be able
get by just fine. However, if you want to make your job a little
sier, you might want to add a few of these to your kitchen:

- **BLENDER** — great for making sauces and purées
- **CHINOIS** — a sieve perfect for straining stocks, sauces, and purées
- **COLANDER** — perfect for straining noodles
- **FOOD PROCESSOR** — the workhorse of the kitchen when it comes mixing, chopping, puréeing, and shredding
- **HAND BLENDER** — great for making sauces and purées right in the pot
- **MANDOLINE** — an extremely sharp utensil used for precise paper-cutting
- **MORTAR and PESTLE** — a stone container and club used to crush spices and herbs

- **RICE COOKER** — an electric gizmo that takes the guessing out of
- **WOK** — a high-sided, sloping, small-bottomed pan — the quintessential Asian utensil

BASIC FOOD SUBSTITUTIONS

If you're in a country like the USA, you might not be able to find an ingredient that a recipe calls for. When this happens, it is usually a good idea to google the ingredient, and find alternative you can get your hands on. Below are a few of such ingredients. you come across more, google is your friend.

THAI INGREDIENT	SUBSTITUTION
Fish sauce	Soy sauce
Cilantro	Parsley
Kaffir lime leaves	Lime peel
Lemongrass	Lemon peel
Rice vinegar	Dry sherry or white vinegar
Long beans	Green beans
Thai eggplant	Green peas
Shallots	Small onions
Homemade curry paste	Store-bought curry paste

THAI CURRY PASTES, MARINADES, AND OTHER CONCOCTIONS

ASIAN MARINADE — 1

Ingredients:

- ¼ cup fish sauce
- ¼ cup soy sauce (if possible low-sodium)
- ½ cup freshly squeezed lime juice
- 1 tablespoon curry powder
- 1 tablespoon light brown sugar
- 1 teaspoon minced garlic Crushed dried red pepper
- 2 tablespoons crispy peanut butter

Directions:

1. Mix all the ingredients in a blender or food processor and pulse until the desired smoothness is achieved.

Yield: Approximately 1¼ cups

ASIAN MARINADE — 2

Ingredients:

- ¼ cup chopped green onion
- ¼ cup soy sauce
- ¼ teaspoon ground anise
- ½ cup lime juice
- 1 tablespoon freshly grated gingerroot
- 1 tablespoon honey
- 1 teaspoon Chinese 5-spice powder
- 2 tablespoons hoisin sauce
- 2 tablespoons sesame oil
- 3 cloves garlic, minced
- 3 tablespoons chopped cilantro
- cup vegetable oil

Directions:

1. Mix the lime juice, soy sauce, hoisin sauce, and honey, and blend thoroughly.
2. Slowly whisk in the vegetable and sesame oils. Put in the rest of the ingredients and mix meticulously.

Yield: Approximately 1¼ cups

This recipe has a definite Chinese influence, featuring soy sauce, hoisin sauce, 5-spice powder, and sesame oil.

BLACK BEAN PASTE

Ingredients:

- 1 medium to big onion, minced
- 1 tablespoon fish sauce
- 1 teaspoon brown sugar
- 2 cloves garlic, chopped
- 2 jalapeños, seeded and chopped
- 2 tablespoons vegetable oil
- 2 teaspoons lime juice
- 3 green onions, trimmed and cut
- 4 tablespoons canned black beans or black soy beans

Directions:

1. In a moderate-sized-sized sauté pan, heat the oil over moderate-the onions, jalapeños, garlic, and green onions, and sauté onion becomes translucent.
2. Using a slotted spoon, move the sautéed vegetables to processor or blender (set aside the oil in the sauté pan). rest of the ingredients and process for a short period of time to create a not-paste.
3. Reheat the reserved oil in the sauté pan. Move the paste and heat for five minutes, stirring continuously. If the paste seems thick, add a small amount of water.

Yield: Approximately ½ cup

HILI TAMARIND PASTE

gredients:

- ½ cup dried shrimp
- 1 cup cut shallots
- 1 tablespoon fish sauce
- 1¾ cups vegetable oil, divided
- 12 small Thai chilies or
- 3 tablespoons brown sugar
- 3 tablespoons Tamarind Concentrate (Page 30)
- 6 serrano chilies
- cup garlic

rections:

1. Put the dried shrimp in a small container. Cover the shrimp stir for a short period of time, and drain; set aside.
2. Pour 1½ cups of the vegetable oil in a moderate-sized deep cooking pan. the oil to roughly 360 degrees on moderate to high heat.
3. Put in the garlic and fry until a golden-brown colour is achieved. Using a slotted move the garlic to a container lined using paper towels.
4. Put in the shallots to the deep cooking pan and fry for two to three minutes; the shallots to the container with the garlic.

5. Fry the reserved shrimp in the deep cooking pan for a couple of minutes; the container.
6. Fry the chilies until they become brittle, approximately h: a minute; them to the container. (Allow oil to cool completely discarding.)
7. Mix the fried ingredients, the rest of the oil, and the a foc processor; process to make a smooth paste.
8. Put the paste in a small deep cooking pan on moderate heat. Put in the sugar and fish sauce, and cook, stirring once in a while, for approximately five minutes.
9. Allow the paste to return to room temperature before placing in an airtight container.

Yield: Approximately 3 cups

CHILI VINEGAR

Ingredients:

- ½ cup white vinegar
- 2 teaspoons fish sauce
- 3 serrano chilies, seeded and finely cut

Directions:

1. Put all of the ingredients in a container.
2. Allow to sit minimum twenty minutes to allow the flavors to develop.

Yield: Approximately ½ cup

COCONUT MARINADE

Ingredients:

- ¼–½ teaspoon red chili pepper flakes
- 1 tablespoon grated lime zest
- 1 tablespoon minced fresh ginger
- 2 tablespoons shredded, unsweetened coconut
- 2 teaspoons sugar
- 3 tablespoons lime juice
- 3 tablespoons rice wine vinegar
- teaspoon curry powder

Directions:

1. Warm the vinegar using low heat. Put in the coconut and ginger to become tender.
2. Turn off the heat and mix in the rest of the ingredients.

Yield: Approximately ½ cup

GREEN CURRY PASTE — 1

Ingredients:

- ¼ cup vegetable oil

- ½ cup chopped cilantro
- ½ teaspoon ground cloves
- ½ teaspoon shrimp paste
- 1 (1½-inch) piece gingerroot, peeled and chopped
- 1 stalk lemongrass, tough outer leaves removed, inner soft portion chopped
- 1 teaspoon black pepper
- 1 teaspoon ground cumin
- 1 teaspoon salt
- 10 green serrano chilies
- 2 teaspoons grated lime zest
- 2 teaspoons ground coriander
- 2 teaspoons ground nutmeg
- 3 shallots, crudely chopped
- 5 cloves garlic

Directions:

1. Put the first 6 ingredients in a food processor and process mixed. Put in the rest of the ingredients, apart from the vegetable process until the desired smoothness is achieved.
2. Slowly put in the oil until a thick paste May be placed in the fridge up to 4 weeks.

Yield: 1 cup

GREEN CURRY PASTE — 2

Ingredients:

- 1 (1-inch) piece ginger, peeled and chopped
- 1 medium onion, chopped
- 1 teaspoon salt
- 1 teaspoon shrimp paste
- 2 green bell peppers, seeded and chopped
- 2 tablespoons vegetable oil
- 2 teaspoons chopped lemongrass
- 2 teaspoons cumin seeds, toasted
- 2–4 green jalapeño chilies, seeded and chopped
- 3 cloves garlic, chopped
- 3 tablespoons coriander seeds, toasted
- 3 teaspoons water
- 4 tablespoons chopped cilantro
- 4 tablespoons Tamarind Concentrate (Page 30)

Directions:

1. Put all the ingredients in a food processor and pulse until the desired smoothness is achieved. Move to a small deep cooking pan and bring to a simmer on moderate to low heat. Decrease the heat to low and cook, stirring regularly, for five minutes.

2. Mix in 1 cup of water and bring the mixture to its boiling point. Decrease the heat, cover, and simmer for half an hour

Yield: Approximately 1 cup

LEMON CHILI VINEGAR

Ingredients:

- 1 quart white wine vinegar Peel of 4 limes
- 8–10 serrano chilies

Directions:

1. Mix all the ingredients in a moderate-sized deep cooking pan and bring to a simmer on moderate heat.
2. Decrease the heat and simmer for about ten minutes.
3. Cool to room temperature, then strain.

Yield: Approximately 1 quart

LEMONGRASS MARINADE

Ingredients:

- ¼ tablespoon soy sauce
- 1 cup extra-virgin olive oil

- 1 jalapeño chili pepper, seeded and chopped
- 1 tablespoon fish sauce
- 2 cloves garlic, minced
- 2 stalks lemongrass, trimmed and smashed
- 2 tablespoons chopped cilantro
- 2 tablespoons lime juice

Directions:

1. Pour the olive oil into a pan and heat until warm.
2. Put in the lemongrass and garlic, and cook for a minute. Turn off the heat and let cool completely.
3. Mix in the rest of the ingredients.

Yield: Approximately 1 cups

MALAYSIAN MARINADE

Ingredients:

- ¼ cup chopped cilantro
- ¼ cup soy sauce
- ¼ cup vegetable oil
- ½ teaspoon coriander
- ½ teaspoon ground cumin
- 1 green onion, trimmed and thinly cut
- 1 teaspoon grated lime zest

- 2 tablespoons grated gingerroot
- 2 tablespoons honey
- 3 tablespoons lime juice

Directions:

1. Mix the honey, lime juice, lime zest, and soy sauce in a small container.
2. Slowly whisk in the oil.
3. Mix in the rest of the ingredients.

Yield: Approximately 1 cup

MINTY TAMARIND PASTE

Ingredients:

- ¼ cup peanuts
- ½ cup Tamarind Concentrate (Page 30)
- 1 bunch cilantro leaves
- 1 bunch mint leaves
- 4–5 Thai bird peppers or 2 serrano chilies, seeded and chopped

Directions:

1. Put all the ingredients in a food processor and pulse to make a paste.

Yield: Approximately 2 cups

NORTHERN (OR JUNGLE) CURRY PASTE

Ingredients:

- ¼ cup chopped arugula
- ¼ cup chopped chives
- ½ cup chopped mint
- 1 (3-inch) piece ginger, peeled and chopped
- 1 cup chopped basil
- 1 stalk lemongrass, tough outer leaves removed and discarded, inner core minced
- 1 tablespoon shrimp paste
- 12 serrano chilies, seeded and chopped
- 2 tablespoons vegetable oil
- 4 shallots, chopped
- 6–8 Thai bird chilies, seeded and chopped

Directions:

1. In a moderate-sized-sized sauté pan, heat the oil on medium. Put in shrimp paste, lemongrass, ginger, and shallots, and sauté until shallots start to turn translucent and the mixture is very aromatic.

2. Move the mixture to a food processor and pulse until adding 1 or 2 tablespoons of water to help with the grinding.
3. Put in the rest of the ingredients and more water if required to pulse until crudely mixed.

Yield: Approximately 2 cups

RED CURRY PASTE — 1

Ingredients:

- 1 (½-inch) piece ginger, finely chopped
- 1 medium onion, chopped
- 1 stalk lemongrass, outer leaves removed and discarded, inner core finely chopped
- 1 teaspoon salt
- 2 garlic cloves, chopped
- 2 tablespoons Tamarind Concentrate (Page 30)
- 2 teaspoons cumin seeds, toasted
- 2 teaspoons paprika
- 3 kaffir lime leaves or the peel of 1 lime, chopped
- 3 tablespoons coriander seeds, toasted
- 3 tablespoons vegetable oil
- 4 tablespoons water
- 6–8 red serrano chilies, seeded and chopped

Directions:

1. Put all the ingredients in a food processor and pulse until super smooth.
2. Move to a small deep cooking pan and bring to a simmer on moderate to low heat. Decrease the heat to low and cook, stirring regularly, for five minutes.
3. Mix in 1 cup of water and bring the mixture to its boiling point. Decrease the heat, cover, and simmer thirty minutes.

Yield: Approximately ½ cup

RED CURRY PASTE — 2

Ingredients:

- 1 (2-inch) piece ginger, peeled and thoroughly minced
- 1 small onion, chopped
- 2 cloves garlic, minced
- 2 stalks lemongrass, tough outer leaves removed and discarded, inner core thoroughly minced
- 2 tablespoons ground turmeric
- 3 big dried red California chilies, seeded and chopped
- 5 dried Thai bird or similar chilies, seeded and chopped

Directions:

1. Put the chilies in a container and cover them with hot water. Allow to stand for minimum 30 minutes. Drain the chilies, saving for later 1 cup of the soaking liquid.
2. Put all the ingredients and 2–3 tablespoons of the soaking liquid in a food processor. Process to make a thick, smooth paste. Put in additional liquid if required.

Yield: Approximately 1 cup

SHREDDED FRESH COCONUT

Ingredients:

- 1 heavy coconut, with liquid

Directions:

1. Preheat your oven to 400 degrees.
2. Pierce the eye of the coconut using a metal skewer or screwdriver and drain the coconut water (reserve it for later use if you prefer).
3. Bake the coconut for fifteen minutes, then remove and allow to cool.
4. When the coconut is sufficiently cool to handle, use a hammer to break the shell. Using the tip of a knife, cautiously pull the flesh from the shell. Remove any remaining brown membrane with a vegetable peeler.

5. Shred the coconut using a 4-sided grater. Fresh coconut will keep in your fridge for maximum one week.

eld: Approximately 1 cup

OUTHERN (OR MASSAMAN) CURRY ASTE

gredients:

- ¼ teaspoon ground cinnamon
- ¼ teaspoon whole black peppercorns
- ½ teaspoon cardamom seeds, toasted
- 1 (1-inch) piece ginger, peeled and minced
- 1 stalk lemongrass, tough outer leaves removed and discarded, inner core finely chopped
- 1 teaspoon lime peel
- 1 teaspoon salt
- 1 teaspoon shrimp paste (not necessary)
- 2 tablespoons coriander seeds, toasted
- 2 tablespoons vegetable oil
- 2 teaspoons brown sugar
- 2 teaspoons cumin seeds, toasted
- 2 whole cloves
- 3 tablespoons Tamarind Concentrate (Page 30)
- 3 tablespoons water

- 6–8 big dried red chilies (often called California chilies), soaked in hot water for five minutes and drained

Directions:

1. Put all ingredients in a food processor and pulse until the desired smoothness is achieved.
2. Move to a small deep cooking pan and bring to a simmer on moderate to low heat. Decrease the heat to low and cook, stirring regularly, for five minutes.
3. Mix in 1 cup of water and bring the mixture to its boiling point. Decrease the heat, cover, and simmer thirty minutes.

Yield: Approximately 1 cup

TAMARIND CONCENTRATE

Ingredients:

- 1 cup warm water
- 2 ounces seedless tamarind pulp (sold in Asian markets)

Directions:

1. Put the tamarind pulp and water in a small container for about twenty minutes or until the pulp is tender.
2. Break the pulp apart using the backside of a spoon and sti until blended.

3. Pour the mixture through a fine-mesh sieve, pushing the tender pulp through the strainer. Discard any fibrous pulp remaining in the strainer.

Yield: Approximately 1 cup

TAMARIND MARINADE

Ingredients:

- ¼ cup fresh lime juice
- ¼ cup toasted, unsweetened coconut
- ¼ cup vegetable oil
- ½ cup chopped cilantro leaves
- 1 shallot, chopped
- 1 tablespoon brown sugar
- 1 tablespoon diced fresh gingerroot
- 1 tablespoon soy sauce
- 1½ cups Tamarind Concentrate (Page 30)
- 2 garlic cloves, minced
- 4 pieces lime peel (roughly ½-inch by two-inches)

Directions:

1. Mix the tamarind and lime peel in a small deep cooking pan and bring to a simmer; cook for five minutes.

2. Turn off the heat and cool completely. Mix in the rest of the ingredients.

Yield: Approximately 2 cups

THAI GRILLING RUB

Ingredients:

- 1 teaspoon dried lime peel
- 1 teaspoon freshly ground black pepper
- 1 teaspoon ground ginger
- 4 teaspoons salt

Directions:

1. Mix all the ingredients and mix meticulously. Store in an airtight container.
2. To use, wash the meat of your choice under cool water and pat dry; drizzle the meat with the spice mixture (to taste) and rub it in together with some olive oil, then grill or broil to your preference.

Yield: Approximately

THAI MARINADE — 1

Ingredients:

- ¼ cup chopped cilantro
- ¼ cup fresh lime juice
- ¼ teaspoon hot pepper flakes
- ½ cup sesame oil
- 1 big stalk lemongrass, crushed
- 1 tablespoon brown sugar
- 2 tablespoons chopped peanuts
- 2 tablespoons fish sauce
- 3 cloves garlic, minced

Directions:

1. Mix the fish sauce and lime juice in a small container.
2. Slowly whisk in the sesame oil, then mix in rest of the ingredients.

Yield: Approximately 1 cup

THAI MARINADE — 2

Ingredients:

- ¼ cup chopped basil leaves
- ¼ cup chopped mint leaves
- ¼ cup peanut oil
- ½ cup rice wine
- 1 small onion, chopped

- 1 tablespoon chopped gingerroot
- 1 tablespoon sweet soy sauce
- 2 tablespoons chopped lemongrass
- 3 cloves garlic, minced
- 3 tablespoons fish sauce

Directions:

1. Mix the fish sauce, sweet soy sauce, and the rice wine in a small container.
2. Slowly whisk in the peanut oil, then mix in rest of the ingredients.

Yield: Approximately 1½ cups

THAI MARINADE — 3

Ingredients:

- ¼ cup chopped cilantro leaves
- ¼ cup lime juice
- ½ cup Red Curry Paste (see recipes on pages 4 and 5)
- 1 (12-ounce) can coconut milk
- 1 stalk lemongrass, roughly chopped
- 1 tablespoon sweet soy sauce
- 1 teaspoon fresh gingerroot, chopped
- 2 tablespoons fish sauce

- 6 kaffir lime leaves, finely cut

ections:

1. Mix the coconut milk, curry paste, lemongrass, and kaffir leaves in a small deep cooking pan; bring to a simmer on moderate heat.
2. Decrease the heat and carry on simmering for fifteen minutes.
3. Turn off the heat and let cool to room temperature.
4. Mix in all the rest of the ingredients.

eld: Approximately 2 cups

HAI VINEGAR MARINADE

gredients:

- ¼ cup chopped lemongrass
- 1 tablespoon fresh grated gingerroot
- 1 tablespoon sugar
- 2–3 tablespoons vegetable oil
- 3 tablespoons chopped green onion
- 3½ cups rice wine vinegar
- 4 cloves garlic, minced
- 6 dried red chilies, seeded and crumbled

rections:

1. Put the garlic, chilies, green onions, and ginger in a food processor or blender and process to make a paste.
2. Heat the oil in a wok or frying pan, put in the paste, and stir-fry for four to five minutes. Turn off the heat and allo the mixture to cool completely.
3. In a small deep cooking pan, bring the vinegar to its boilir point. Put in the sugar and the lemongrass; decrease the heat and simmer for about twenty minutes.
4. Mix in the reserved paste.

Yield: Approximately 3 cups

YELLOW BEAN SAUCE

Ingredients:

- 1 (½-inch) piece ginger, peeled and chopped
- 1 medium to big onion, minced
- 1 teaspoon ground coriander
- 2 serrano chilies, seeded and chopped
- 2 tablespoons lime juice
- 2 tablespoons vegetable oil
- 2 tablespoons water
- 4 tablespoons fermented yellow beans (fermented soy beans)

Directions:

1. In a moderate-sized-sized sauté pan, heat the oil on moderate heat. Put in the onion and chilies, and sauté until the onion becomes translucent. Mix in the ginger and coriander, and carry on cooking for half a minute.
2. Put in the beans, lime juice, and water, and simmer using low heat for about ten minutes.
3. Move the mixture to a blender and process until the desired smoothness is achieved.

Yield: Approximately 1 cup

ABOUT THE AUTHOR

Born and brought up in Thailand, Urassaya Manaying is a professional cook and nutritionist who specializes in traditional Thai recipes. She is best known for her cookbooks on Thai Cooking.

Printed in Great Britain
by Amazon